Tales from the Dog Park

By Melinda Dille
Art by Clinton Banbury

HARVEST HOUSE PUBLISHERS

EUGENE, OREGON

Cover and interior design by Franke Design and Illustration, Minneapolis, Minnesota

TALES FROM THE DOG PARK
Copyright © 2008 text by Melinda Dille; artwork by Clinton Banbury
Published by Harvest House Publishers
Eugene, Oregon 97402
www.harvesthousepublishers.com
ISBN-13: 978-0-7369-2099-5
ISBN-10: 0-7369-2099-4

To all my two- and four-legged loved ones. You know who you are!

And to dog and pet lovers: I hope you enjoy reading every page
as much as I loved writing it. May this book be an instrument of joy
along life's path. God bless.

May we all love one another as God loves us.

—Melinda

ACKNOWLEDGMENTS

Thank you to these friends who without
their help, love, and assistance I wouldn't be
sharing this book with you.

To my two-legged angels: You are true gifts from God. I thank Him every day
for you: Cari Ingrassia, Liz Cawood, Dana Turell, Robin Race, Jean Christen,
Virginia Register, Jeff Wagner, Jim Han, Barry McQueen, and David Loveall.

To my four-legged friends: My inspiration, my heart beat—Jingles and Ubee;
the dogs of Alton Baker, Amazon, and Wayne Morse dog parks; the dogs of
Avalon Village; and all of the great dogs I encounter daily. And I never forget
those that now play in the green fields of heaven.

May we love dogs as much as they love us.

—Melinda

With thanks to Zoë for her love and Fairfax and Wilbur for their inspiration.

—Clint

CONTENTS

1. Hang Loose

Go with the flow. When I think of this little phrase of wisdom, I think about two great dogs I had in my life about 20 years ago. Sophie and Snuffy were bassett hounds. If you have ever been around this breed, you know they are truly a hang-loose type of dog—not only in their skin, but also in their attitudes. They are like an old-fashioned dog pull toy, just going with the flow, slinking and sliding over any obstacle without complaining. Every day is a vacation to a bassett. They take life as it comes and don't get too upset over much. For my two gentle, happy dogs, even going to the vet was no big deal.

Unfortunately, people sometimes get so wrapped up in unimportant things that when significant happenings do arise, we become Chicken Littles hollering "The sky is falling!" And when we are sure our sky is falling every day, people stop listening to our cries. Our busy lives lead us to be hypersensitive and uptight. But if we take our cues from Sophie and Snuffy, we can learn to take life as it comes and receive each good time and hard time with gratitude. Hanging loose means releasing our grip on every moment. We can't control life as it unfolds, but we can learn to experience the rush of delight as it continues.

Happiness is a warm puppy.

Charles Schulz

2. Love Comes in All Sizes

Little Jingles is a 15-year-old, 18-pound doxie/terrier mix. Jingles was so fortunate to share my home with Ubee (who sadly isn't with me any longer). Ubee was a big rottweiler/shepherd with a huge heart. Jingles became a bit spoiled and began to think he too was a large dog. Ubee was always gracious enough to let Jingles play along and keep that big dog attitude.

One sunny day a young Great Dane (100 pounds) took a liking to my little Jingles. Nothing could keep that big dog from him. He lavished Jingles with kisses or what I would call a long tongue bath. It was an adorable hour of laughs for everyone at the dog park. This Great Dane was following little Jingles everywhere. He literally only had eyes for my little guy. When the Great Dane and his person left the dog park, the dog kept looking back to see Jingles until he was out of sight.

Nobody could believe this dog-park case of love at first sight. Well, nobody except Jingles...who expected love because he'd been spoiled by Ubee.

9

3. Open Doors

There they are just up ahead—those double gates to the dog park that signal playtime. Beyond them is a field where fur can fly and canines can be themselves. Those doors offer freedom and joy, but the ones leading to animal shelters offer confinement and fear. Sadly, many dogs must face the latter because their humans failed to see them as living, loving creatures needing time, love, and care.

Chance is one of those dogs. He's a handsome dalmatian who was adopted as a puppy when a certain movie's popularity inspired countless folks to bring spotted wonders into their homes. Many people paid big money for puppies only to discover that severe health issues can sometimes emerge with this breed. Suddenly these happy, iconic dogs started showing up in shelters. Chance is deaf, and he, like many others, was left sad, lonely, and bewildered.

Dogs and other pets are not accessories or fashion statements (though they seem to enhance the appearance of more than a few female celebrities). Animals are flawed and yet completely loveable, just like we are. When they see the open door up ahead, they too hope it is one that leads to unconditional love and good times. And as Chance's sweet name implies...most of all we and our dogs are really hoping for more opportunities to love.

A dog can express more with his tail
in minutes than his owner can
express with his tongue in hours.

Anonymous

4. Say No to Leashes

The most obedient of dogs seems to change personality the instant its leash comes off. At the dog park I have seen the most dramatic transformation with a simple snap of the leash. No longer are dogs being held back by the lumbering human on the other end of the leather strap. They could care less that being tethered to a person often keeps them safe. They want to feel the ease of that restriction and have a free pass to frolic! Most of the dogs run, play, and run some more, never tiring of their freedom. At the end of a day at the dog park, I've witnessed canines run the other direction when they see their human partners holding the leash and calling out, "Time to go home!"

People might not have gemstone collars, but we do have leashes that keep us where we are, not allowing us to go too far out. Some people control their own leash, while others seem to invite everyone else to take control so they don't have to make decisions. If you control the leashes of others in your life, I say let them go. This doesn't mean you want people to end up running into trouble, but it does mean you can release yourself from the pressure of making sure everybody does what he or she is supposed to do.

12

Like the fences that border the dog park, the boundaries in our own lives keep us safe. But if you feel held back from dreams, love, acceptance, or goals, or if you feel stuck in a bad job or relationship, it's time to examine who's on the controlling end of your life. Often it is through simple decisions that we free ourselves from those people or obligations that keep our lives limited and held back. The sooner you realize that only God is truly in control, the sooner you can say "no" to those worldly things that tie you down. Then you can say "yes" to your purpose and direction with freedom.

13

5. Those Are Barkin' Words

Whenever Ubee came across a dog in a bad mood, she let him have it—with kindness and a few instructive barks to buck up. It was her nature to rally everyone else around her to happiness. Jingles, on the other hand, just turns and walks the other way. He knows that a bad mood might erupt into a confrontation, and truly he is a lover, not a fighter.

Some of the loudest barks I've ever heard have come from my two-legged friends suffering from cranky dispositions. And usually their barks are inflicted upon people who had nothing to do with the problem. They are just in the wrong place at the wrong time.

Haven't we all experienced that dilemma? What do you do? Do you back off or do you strut forward and enter the fray?

And when you're in a bad mood, do you become a barker? Or do you find a way to release your pent-up negativity in a positive way? Life is tough. Bad moods will trip us all up in our quest to be perfect friends. Tough situations will arise, and we need to decide how we want to handle them. Next time you sense a cloud covering your mind-set, do what our canine teachers suggest—take a walk. Not only is it good for the body, it does wonders for the spirit.

6. All About Me?

Dogs are so good at communicating what they want: Throw the ball, scratch me, hug me, let me out, feed me, take me to the dog park, give me a bath, and love me all of the time. As loving as our pets are, they also express a perspective that life is all about them when they are communicating their needs. There's a long list of dogs in my life—Jingles, Patton, Fergus, Bailey, Kiva, and Benny—who remind me of this quality frequently. What can we take from this "me, me, me" mantra without becoming self-absorbed?

Most people struggle to communicate what they want and need because they don't know what they want or need. We often spend our time and resources caring for someone else. It is difficult to switch gears and understand that we have needs for nurturing, play, and friendship too. We have too much to juggle to add our own stuff to the mix. Right? Moms are a great example of people who do so much for others. Their jobs are endless, going from sunup to sundown and beyond. This labor comes from a place of tireless love, but eventually we all grow weary if we're not being energized and refilled. Maybe we should never cross over to the way of "me, me, me," but we can examine our needs, seek nurturing through faith, and ask for a hug now and then.

7. Make a New Friend

Jingles loves springtime. It's the perfect season—it isn't too cold or too hot. It's just right! The arrival of spring is a great time to get outside, explore, and make new friends—especially at our favorite dog parks. Everyone Jingles and I encounter is so nice and seems genuinely happy to see us after the long winter. Some people even welcome the opportunity to say hello. It's wonderful how dogs help bring people together.

When I first moved to Oregon from California, I was facing the excitement and the difficulties of transition. With mixed emotions and lots of prayer, I walked forward and tried not to look back. One day I spotted a wonderful housing development, and all of a sudden I knew I wanted to be a homeowner again. I wasn't sure I would qualify to finance one of these homes, but I kept praying. I also conferred with Ubee and Jingles about the decision. I even promised that if we got the house I would walk them every day in the new neighborhood.

God answered my prayer with a resounding "Yes!" And, as promised, I walked Jingles and Ubee every day. Filled with the joy of this blessing, I expressed my happiness and friendliness to everyone I encountered on those strolls. One person I got to know was my next-door neighbor Virginia. We exchanged waves and hellos, and eventually she asked me about my dogs and my life. From those curbside chats a wonderful friendship was born. She recently recalled that when she first saw me with the two dogs walking in freezing weather she thought I was off my rocker. But once she got to know me and my story, she understood.

Sometimes gratitude leads us to do things we wouldn't normally do. And wouldn't ya know it...when we fulfill those promises we make out of a grateful heart, we are often led to even more wonders—like the gift of friendship.

8. A New Day

Every day is a clean slate in the doggy mind. Our furry friends are blessed with short memory spans (except when it comes to locating dirty chew toys buried last fall). Jingles, a happy little dog, jumps up in the morning and welcomes a new day. He isn't remembering that Rupert the cat scratched him last night or that the vet visit was less than pleasant.

People, unlike dogs, have big memory banks. And some of those banks hold empty or negative deposits. We store things and sometimes just can't move on. If the problems of the past are still bugging you, I invite you to do what dogs do—live in the moment. Experience today in all its newness, freshness, and beauty. It could turn out to be the best day ever. And who knows what surprises it will offer!

As the old saying goes, "Yesterday is yesterday; we can't change anything about it. And we don't know what tomorrow holds. But today we can treat ourselves to the pure joy of a new day, a new beginning."

9. The Pleasures of the Shallow End

Some summer days are just plain blazing, and those days create many a hot dog! At the dog park there are always lots of wading pools filled with cold, clear water just waiting for frisky, hot dogs to jump into. It is always entertaining to watch the scene that unfolds around and in the shallow end. Some tiptoe around the edge and, believe it or not, exhibit true human behavior. I just know they are thinking, "Should I? Shouldn't I? Is this really allowed?" Some dogs jump in full-bodied and immerse themselves as fast as possible. These tend to be the ones who don't mind a crowd. It's a pool party after all!

I grew up in a neighborhood with lots of kids running everywhere. Summertime was our season of pure adventure, fun, and seeking out the cool spots (literally!). The Ceglia family had an above-the-ground pool that was just right for all of us to play in—and the more the merrier. We put that pool to the test every summer day. I have pictures of us in this pool all crouched down so no one could see our suits, and all you can see are little faces with rubber swim caps on. Swim caps in a wading pool? Those were the days! And then one summer came the introduction of the Slip 'N Slide. It was the invention of all inventions! The pool and Slip 'N Slide parties went on for days until someone got hurt or the power struggles of who got to go in first took over the fun. But usually the next day, or week, and certainly by the next summer, we all were more than eager to get right back into the cool fun.

When it's hot, dig deep and let the kid come out. Head to the lake, beach, river, or pool. It's time to cool off. And don't forget to invite your four-legged friends to jump right in with you!

10. Bask in Your Greatness

My friend Carol's dog, Murphy, is one of those dogs who was born with an air of greatness. He knows it is vital to be a big part of anything and everything Carol does. After all, he's the main attraction, right? If Carol heads for the lake, Murphy is right there watching like a star lifeguard. And when she goes windsurfing, Murphy is waiting at the shoreline for her while taking pats on the head and praise from those passing by who are quick to tell him he is a great dog. He laps it up every time and never with an attitude, only with humble gratefulness.

Often the truly great people in our lives are the most humble, the most giving, and the least aware of their goodness. These people never show up with an attitude when they are there to support you and cheer you on. You can probably list a few folks like this. At least I hope you can. And while you might not admit it, you're likely one of these people too. We tend to see the success and ability and charm of others, but we forget to see our own unique greatness. We need to remember to tell others how great they are, and, like Murphy, we need to accept kind words from friends and strangers and a few pats on the back.

You do not own a dog,
the dog owns you.

Author Unknown

25

11. Respect Your Elders

At the dog park age differences are pretty visible. Young dogs will run over to an older dog and often get a most unpleasant welcome for their rambunctious behavior. Sometimes the older one will just ignore the young one. Then there are those senior dogs that can really put a young one in its place. My Ubee was like that. I've seen some young dogs just shake it off and run to terrorize another dog. Sometimes though, a young dog chooses to hang out with the older one. It's interesting how the young dog emulates what the more mature dog does, trying to get approval while also showing respect by being kinder and gentler with this mentor than with its own peers. The two become friends.

In the neighborhood where my office is, I recently observed a college student walking with a very old dog. He was very slow and clearly blind. The young woman had on running clothes, but she chose to walk slowly to keep pace with her companion. I noticed when he stopped to rest she would stop and look around at the trees to give him time. Maybe she was listening to the sounds of the neighborhood. Perhaps her mind was a million miles away. One thing was certain—she was enjoying her day with her older friend. Life can't get much better!

There is so much to be learned from those who've lived longer. Let's take a moment to slow down, stop, recognize, and accept the great value of emulating the ways of our mature friends and the many wonders that their pace exposes to our own senses.

12. Be Thankful

Every day is a blessing. In our rushed state of living we can overlook that blessing like we might miss seeing a four-leaf clover. Our pet children are thankful and appreciative for even the simplest things like daily food, fresh water, and a nice blanket. They remind us to be equally grateful. After a hearty meal, Jingles jumps up on the couch, settles into his warm blanket, and looks up at me as if to say, "Thanks for taking such good care of me!" In a dog's life it is the small things that are welcome.

The distractions of busyness, obligations, and our worries can keep us from seeing the little blessings that help our lives along. We miss out on the contentment of consistent gifts that enhance and enrich our lives.

Maybe a lot of us do need to go back to kindergarten to learn something that is innate in dogs (or learned during the first days of obedience school): It is always right to say "please" and "thank you" and mean it. What kindnesses have you overlooked? What daily contributions do others make to the functioning of your life? Even when we are enjoying the basic needs like food and shelter, we should always be thankful when receiving them.

My goal in life is to become as
wonderful as my dog thinks I am.

Toby & Eileen Green

29

13. Keep Going

In people years, Ubee lived to be 98. Wow! And what a life this big, happy girl had. From the time she was a pup to her adulthood, she was challenged with a list of problems. She was born with dual hip displacement and hindered with bad skin allergies and a sensitive stomach. Just one of these ailments could have cut her life short were it not for her positive outlook. She met everything head-on with a willingness not only to survive, but to love, love, love life. This fueled her on in great ways, and her life was full and rich.

We can learn about contentment and perseverance from the canine spirit. Sometimes, no matter what, you just have to keep going. Grab the gusto in life and be happy. There will be bumps in the road from time to time. Those are life lessons. Learn and go on. We can complain daily about the things we lack and be blind to everything we have. Or we can use our difficulties as a path to a good life. You can choose to be happy—Ubee happy.

A bend in the road is not
the end of the road...unless you
fail to make the turn.

Author Unknown

14. Accept a Chance to Party!

Ever wonder where the phrase "party animal" came from? I think it comes from the dog park! When one arrives at the dog park, a welcoming committee of various sizes and shapes and breeds greets you. And before you can say hi to them all, your dog has joined the party. There is so much excitement happening. All of the dogs are greeting, sniffing, running, jumping, and playing. They all have smiles on their faces.

At a great party, everyone is happy, laughing, and glad to welcome others into the fold. Fun is in the air. The problems and worries are left at the door. I remember one Fourth of July when my neighbors and I decided to celebrate all weekend long. More and more people showed up, and we kept making room for them.

If you tend to run solo, do yourself a favor and every once in a while join in the pack. Become a party animal who is always willing to make room for more new friends while continuing to celebrate with old friends.

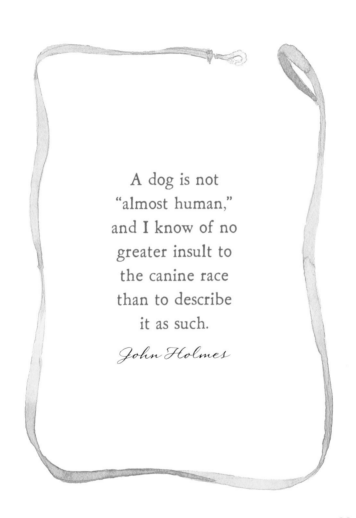

A dog is not
"almost human,"
and I know of no
greater insult to
the canine race
than to describe
it as such.

John Holmes

15. Royal Manners

No matter where you are, good manners will always help you go further.

In the days when kings and queens ruled much of the world, good-mannered dogs were depicted in paintings standing dignified and loved beside their royal owners. And I'm pretty sure that the bad-mannered dogs were left out in the cold to survive on their own.

While we might not be booted out into the cold, we will be more warmly received if we use good manners and treat others with respect. How are your manners in this hurry-up world we live in? Are they like that of a junkyard dog or a regal German shepherd?

Are you willing to graciously serve someone regardless of stature or professional title? You will have a noble heart when you give anyone who crosses your path the royal treatment of good manners.

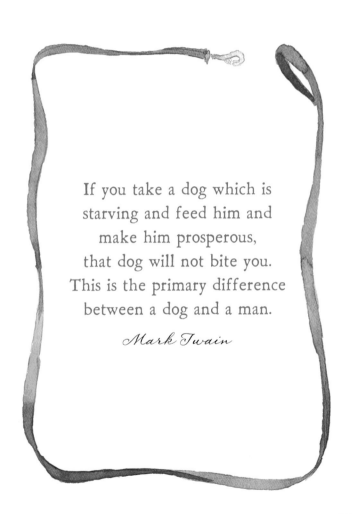

If you take a dog which is
starving and feed him and
make him prosperous,
that dog will not bite you.
This is the primary difference
between a dog and a man.

Mark Twain

16. Just Be Yourself

Dogs don't enter the dog park with hesitation about who they are or whether the collar they are wearing is trendy. Well, sometimes they do keep their eye on another dog's chew toy, but they don't wish they had one just like that or even better...they wish they had *that* toy. And even while a tug-o-war ensues, they are not wishing they were a different breed or had a different personality or nature. Even the shyest of the shy and the boldest of the bold seem perfectly content being their dog selves.

Why do we get so caught up comparing our lives, our toys, and our personalities to those we encounter? And the bigger mystery is, why do we let this comparison alter us as though a slight shift to the left or the right will make us on track to be more accepted and loved?

This week be yourself. Love who you are (many people already do, you know!). And be thankful for what you have. When you enter your next gathering, share who you are with friends and strangers rather than holding tightly to your insecurities. After all, you might need to reach for a chew toy at a moment's notice.

Always hold your head up,
but be careful to hold your
nose at a friendly level.

Max L. Forman

17. It's All About Attitude

I will always remember two great dogs that lived with my sister and her family. Pete and Maryanne were beautiful golden Labs that showed up one day at my sister's home. Her house is in the country, and it is a known fact that many pets, for unreasonable reasons, are dumped in the country. One day these lovely animals made their way to my sister's property. My nephew, Nathan, then about seven, instantly fell in love with these two weary travelers. My sister, Liz, took the tired, thin dogs to a vet right away, where it was determined that this seemingly happy duo had been walking many, many miles. Despite being hungry, neglected, and weak, they had great attitudes and were eager for the expressions of love they received from my sister and nephew. I can still see their wonderful faces, radiant with the joy of finding a good home.

I have a friend who is a great example of living with a positive outlook. He welcomes every day as a great one. I'm sure, like most of us, he has worries (like two trips to the hospital in a year) and disappointments, but he seizes the opportunity to make darker times bright. You just can't help but feel great being around him. I must admit there have been days when I've been less than positive and in need of an attitude adjustment. He is just the person to give me one. And because he's so positive, he doesn't even know how much he's helping me.

When you are tempted to turn the bumps and struggles of your journey into a reason to be angry at the world, take a moment to embrace the new day and the chance to love, be loved, and to make another person's day brighter just by knowing you.

The more people I meet
the more I like my dog.

Author Unknown

18. Live in the Moment

I watch Jingles many mornings during his patrol of our backyard. He isn't really thinking about the nice bowl of food I just prepared for him or that Vinnie the cat is waiting to chase him when he comes back in. He's so focused on the moment.

All of us are running here and there, cell phone in ear, overwhelmed by responsibilities and obligations. Stop! While trying to live our lives, our lives are passing us by. Don't let it pass unnoticed. Here is a poem I wrote to friends and family for Christmas to express the importance of taking time.

Cherish the Moment...

The sun is coming up here in the Northwest...
God has painted a magenta masterpiece of color that
seems to be pushing the gray in the sky away...
It is winter now.
A lone rose branch hulas in the soft morning breeze.
All is calm...
All is quiet...
At this moment...
Let us honor this moment...
Not the last...
Not those to come...
Just this moment of quiet.

Today, right now, pause, take a deep breath, look around.
Find joy in the moment. Do that often for yourself. And share
this idea with a busy friend this week.

19. Get Out and Socialize

It's five o'clock somewhere. At the dog park it's always five o'clock and time to be social. At my dog park, there is a group of people who own rottweilers, and they all meet up. It looks like a convention sometimes with 20 of these beautiful, strong dogs running around playing together. Their owners enjoy their time together as well. The dogs are good about the house rules and even let uninvited dogs join them. Ubee used to. She must've recognized that they were distant relatives and that this social hour was open to all. In no time, she had a pack of new friends.

My friend Dottie has many friends and loves hosting dinner parties. An evening at Dottie's home is like an evening spent at a five-star restaurant. She is gracious, welcoming, and one great cook! When unexpected guests show up, that is no problem for Dottie. She is quick to set another place, pour another glass of wine, and get to know her additional guest.

Do you love to socialize or do you choose the quiet corner of the room? It doesn't really matter as long as you are enjoying yourself and the company of others. What a great way to spend an evening, especially after a dog-tired week of work. And who knows, you might make a new friend or two.

43

20. Some Days You Just Have to Take a Nap

The warmth of summer, the cold of winter—it doesn't matter what the season—every smart dog makes the most of a climate by taking a nap. While I write, Jingles is cozy between two cushions on the couch. He'll nap for a while, and then suddenly he'll wake up frisky and ready to go for the second walk of the day. There's that short memory!

Naps are such a luxury in our hurried lives. Slumbering actually refreshes our minds and bodies. So why don't we stop and rest? Why aren't you taking a break for a nap? Work, chores, and running around are always there. Quite frankly, you won't miss a thing by slowing down and doing something nice for yourself. Today, take a short nap. You'll wake up refreshed, rejuvenated, and ready for another round of work, play, and living. Ahhh...the comforts of a dog's life.

Our dogs, like our shoes, are comfortable.
They might be a bit out of shape and a little
worn around the edges, but they fit well.

Bonnie Wilcox

45

21. Good Grace

There is nothing sweeter than a senior dog. Lady Bug was my dog when I was a young girl. She was a pregnant stray when we took her in. This tiny, terrier-type dog with the littlest legs and I became fast friends. She went through so much in my life with me. She shared the happy times, sad times, and fearful times of my shy preteen life. She even comforted me and, I think, shared wisdom as I experienced my first love. She loved nothing better than going to the beach or lake with us. She lived a happy life. When she passed away, she left us just as she came into our world, naturally and with sweet dignity.

Seniors who are part of our lives have seen and experienced much. They are always aware that mixed with great joy there will be times of sadness, but then joy comes once again. They understand what it means to live richly and appreciate every day. Many times they can't move as fast as they once did or their memories are not what they were. They accept aches and pains and the ups and downs because they have learned to savor all of life.

The flavors of life are truly sweeter for all of us because of the wisdom, guidance, friendship, and presence of the elderly. While we hurry here and there, let's be mindful of these important people and thank them for all they give to us and the community.

A dog doesn't care if you're
rich or poor, big or small,
young or old. He doesn't care
if you're not smart, not popular,
not a good joke-teller,
not the best athlete, nor the
best-looking person. To your
dog, you are the greatest,
the smartest, the nicest human
being who was ever born. You
are his friend and protector.

Louis Sabin, All About Dogs As Pets

22. Forgive and Forget

I was watching a television ministry the other day. The host and guest were talking about forgiving and forgetting. When you ask God for forgiveness, He not only forgives you but forgets that which you asked forgiveness for. The slate is wiped clean.

Many dog lovers will point out that "dog" is "God" spelled backward. Our dogs might not be holy and perfect, but they do offer a divine example of forgiveness. They quickly forget any of our transgressions, like delaying their dinner when we work late or how they got in trouble moments before. After Jingles receives a scolding for eating the cat food (bad Jingles!) he soon is by my side and eager to play.

Many times we'll forgive, but the forgetting is hard. When we leave out this important part of the process, it trips us up over and over. Let's follow the godly and doggy examples in our lives and learn how to embrace true forgiveness.

I think dogs are the most amazing creatures;
they give unconditional love. For me
they are the role model for being alive.

Gilda Radner

23. Take a Holiday

Vacation time is always a great way to renew, refresh, and revive our spirits. When Ubee and Jingles were younger, vacation time meant that these guys got to go to the dog hotel. The minute we turned onto the road where this dog hotel was located, they both went wild with excitement. My feelings could've been a bit hurt by that excitement, but I knew they were just looking forward to being a dog among all of the other dogs and doing the things dogs love to do best—play, sniff, get all wet, dry off in dirt, be on patrol, and eat new food. With their excitement, they jumped out of the car and ran to the open gate. They went straight to the person in charge and didn't even look back. They were truly in vacation mode!

Vacations for humans in yesteryear meant, for the most part, packing up your stuff and heading via car, train, plane, or ship to a welcomed destination that would help take you away from work, worries, and a worn-out spirit. Now we leave our homes but often pack along our cell phones, laptops, and other communication devices and bring all our regular burdens right along with us. If we stay connected to all these "things of home," we never get the absolute joy of a new experience.

On your next vacation, visit places that spark your senses and renew your soul. Eat food you normally don't eat. Follow that person who opens the doors to wonderful adventures and don't look back until that alarm wakes you to go back to work.

With eye upraised his master's look to scan,
The joy, the solace, and the aid of man:
The rich man's guardian and
the poor man's friend,
The only creature faithful to the end.

George Crabbe

24. Let Others Love You

I knew a dog, Ginger, who was truly a one-person dog. She was so protective of her owner that she would bite people who got too close. Many of us tried to get Ginger to accept us, but mostly we had to be on guard when near this bad-mannered dog. Sadly, Ginger's owner passed away and this seemingly sweet snowball of a dog had to work through her attitude in order to love anyone else.

There are plenty of people who, like Ginger, have a hard time trusting more than one person. Their ability to accept love is limited. Someone once shared about a woman who was so critical of others, bitter about hardships, and negative that she'd kept everyone out of her life except for one friend. Thankfully this friend was loyal, but when she passed away, the lonely, hardened woman was left to rebuild relationships she had damaged long ago.

These stories are similar in their sadness, but also in their hopefulness. The good news is that relationships can be rebuilt and that dogs and people can learn how to open up their hearts in new ways. Once the hurdle of fear is overcome, love is often waiting.

Animals are such agreeable friends—
they ask no questions,
they pass no criticisms.

George Eliot

25. Let the Race Begin

I have seen many rescued greyhounds. Most of them are very sweet, but they are always on the move. They see a path up ahead, and they have to take off in pursuit of whatever. It's their competitive nature and training that has made them that way. Many times, larger and stronger dogs just move aside and let the greyhounds pass on by. They look at the greyhounds as if to say, "Aren't you even going to stop and play?"

Have you ever watched people in your life or those on the road zoom by, unwilling to see anything other than their end destinations? This just happened to me last night. I was going the speed limit, but the person behind me just couldn't wait. I decided to pull over and let him pass. What cracked me up is that when I got to the next big intersection, the car that passed me was waiting at the light. In fact, I realized that because the driver had hurried on ahead, he ended up waiting longer at the light.

There will be greyhounds in our lives—people who zoom by and have no interest in visiting, playing, or getting to know us. It's okay. Let them pass so you can continue on your path and at your own sweet pace.

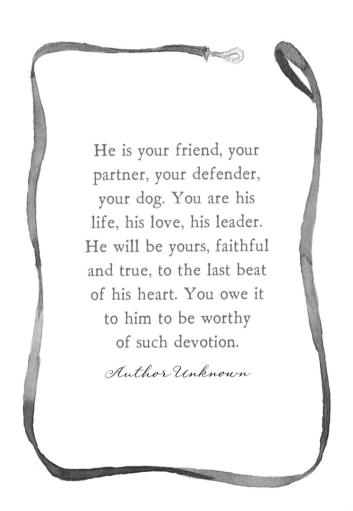

He is your friend, your
partner, your defender,
your dog. You are his
life, his love, his leader.
He will be yours, faithful
and true, to the last beat
of his heart. You owe it
to him to be worthy
of such devotion.

Author Unknown

26. Negotiate Whenever Possible

Dogs are great negotiators, and they aren't even aware of it. Jingles stares at me with his big brown eyes and negotiates an extra dog walk, a little snack, and another blanket among a few other things. I can't say no! It's a fact: Pet people are usually led by their pet's desires.

In the human world we spend a lot of time negotiating, and it requires a lot more than a flash of beautiful brown eyes. When we maneuver lines in the grocery store, or the

busy rows of a shopping center parking lot, or when we set a curfew for teenagers, buy a new car, or ask for a raise, we are negotiating our way through life. When we negotiate the big things, life can be stressful. If it were up to us, we would get our way without having to speak up for what we wanted, or compromise, or change our course to adjust for the plans of others. But take it from the dogs...stand up, look at your desires straight on, and be yourself. Before you know it, you'll walk toward your purpose wagging with confidence.

27. Missing You

I saw a cute cartoon that had a little dog howling while looking out the front window. If I wrote the caption it would say: "Jingles, I'm just going to get the mail." Sometimes I forget how lonely and sad he is when I go off to work. Pets are always happy and grateful for our time. They show us that from their facial expressions to their wagging tails.

We forget how important it is to stay connected to the lives of others. Procrastination and our busy schedules keep us from following through on the tugs at our heart. It's easy to think that maybe tomorrow we will have the chance to pick up the phone and call someone, and then the time passes and the call is never placed. That person may really need to hear from us in that particular moment.

Do you know someone who is howling at the window for just a few minutes of your time? I bet you do. Stop what you're doing right now (which is reading this!), go to the phone, and call him or her. You will make your friend so happy. And you know what? You'll be happy from your head right down to your toes!

59

28. Stand Tall

At the dog park you see the behavior of hierarchy. There always has to be an alpha dog, and sometimes it is a surprise who gets this role. I've witnessed what seems to be the weaker dog finally having enough of the other dog's behavior and surprisingly standing up to the strong dog.

There might be a confrontation of sorts, like showing teeth, but usually the two end up meeting in the middle, hanging out, and playing together.

Humans are like this too. We all encounter bullies in this life. Early on we learn that the sooner we stand up to the bully, the quicker he or she will back down. And sometimes the bully isn't really a bully, but is someone who has lots of insecurities and wants to be noticed.

Remember this: Our backbones were made to be straight, not bent with fear and avoidance. Stand tall against the bullies in your life. Not only will you find out you're stronger than you thought you were, but the other guy will know too!

I am I because my little dog knows me.

Gertrude Stein

29. Good Times

One day I saw a guy and a beagle out for exercise. Nothing new, right? Well, the dog was in the man's backpack. Not only that, but the guy was traveling on rollerblades! They both were having a great time. Who says exercise with your dog has to be boring?

I know right here and now that there is no way to get my Jingles to stay in a backpack or to sit passively in a bike basket, but we do walk our neighborhood every day and love every minute of it together.

So if you have a puppy pal in the backyard who hasn't been out on an excursion with you for a while, grab her and the leash and get going. I guarantee you'll both have fun!

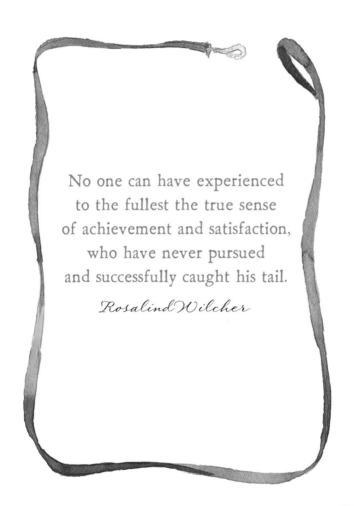

No one can have experienced
to the fullest the true sense
of achievement and satisfaction,
who have never pursued
and successfully caught his tail.

Rosalind Wilcher

30. Let It Go and Move On

Are small things in your life tying you up like a ball of string or tripping you on your way to taking care of bigger things? Even dogs can relate to this. Jingles was enjoying the summer sun minding his own business when suddenly there was a pesky fly zipping around his nose. Jingles would jump up and shake his head to get rid of the pesky bug. As soon as he settled back down, the fly would zip and zoom around him again. I watched this scene and it was like instant replay—about five times. Finally Jingles had all he could take. He got up and moved across the yard.

We can get so caught up in small things that they become big in our minds. Just the other day I had to deal with a minor repair on my car. Before I took it in to be looked at, I had already made up my mind that this auto repair was going to set me back big time. Much to my surprise, it didn't. Yet I had already wound my worries up like a ball of string.

Next time something small comes buzzing into your line of sight, swat it away. If that doesn't work, keep moving until you leave your worries behind.

The one absolutely unselfish friend
that man can have in this selfish
world, the one that never deserts him,
the one that never proves ungrateful
or treacherous, is his dog.

George Graham Vest

31. The Value of a Smile

Scandal was a great dog, an Australian shepherd–Queensland heeler mix. He lived with me throughout my twenties. Being a cattle dog, he always wanted to work. Whether herding up his toys or taking control of the vacuum cleaner, he loved his job. When he got to be around real cattle, he was a natural master herder and protector. The cowboys called him one of the best. His shy ways would quickly melt when people praised him and smiled at his good performance.

I know people who don't like to smile. They think they might lose their business edge if people see them expose a friendly, personal side. Truth is, they would probably go a lot further in business if they embraced their work, their purpose, and their heart's labor with a smile.

Smiling lifts everyone's mood, the giver of smiles and the recipient. Chance encounters with other smiling people can be infectious. We have all been in stressful situations, and then someone smiles and immediately the stress level goes down.

This world would be a nicer one if everyone smiled at one another more often. I know some dogs that agree with me on this fact.

32. Age Is Just Age

Jingles is a walking, running, happy specimen of great health for a 15-year-old dog. He can still keep up with younger and sprier friends at the dog park. One of his best friends is our neighbor's black Lab puppy, Samuel. He and Jingles love chasing each other around the yard. Most of the time Jingles tires Samuel out. (Jingles has the wisdom to know how to pace himself.)

In his retirement years, my brother-in-law and his son hiked the Oregon portion of the Pacific Crest Trail. This is not a trek to be done by novices or without a lot of preparation. It took them a month to do the hike. They experienced all kinds of weather, and I think the older of the two was probably better at pacing himself. The gift of age came in handy on this memorable trip.

Some pups and humans choose to sit on the couch and let life go by. There is always tomorrow in their minds. How are you living your life? How is your dog living his or her life? There's no time like the present to make a change and grab the gusto!

33. Face Fear Straight On

I have known many vets, and they are all very nice people. But it's their patients' wish to see them at the dog park, not in the office for professional reasons. Any dog who has had his basic health care visits knows that the sign to the vet's office means they're going to get prodded and examined. To them I say, "Be brave, little guys. You don't realize it, but it's for your own good. Soon you'll be returned to the comfort of your home." With my encouragement, my dog makes it through the visit every time.

People and their doctors seem to have the same relationship. Many patients would rather see their doctors on the golf course than in the medical office. So often people allow their fear of something "bad" happening to stop them from moving forward, gathering information, and seeing what life has to offer.

As we all know, life is tough. Many times we want to run and hide under the bed because we are so fearful. But eventually we have to get out and face the fear. I've faced many fearful things, and I'm happy to report that I'm still here to say that when you face fear straight on it feels so empowering.

What holds you back in this life? Maybe it's time for a checkup. Once you examine your fears, you'll realize that they're nothing that faith and a little encouragement won't see you through.

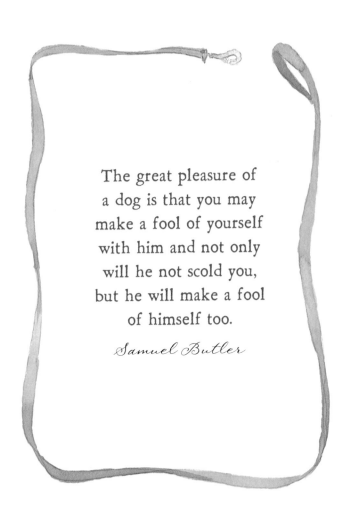

The great pleasure of
a dog is that you may
make a fool of yourself
with him and not only
will he not scold you,
but he will make a fool
of himself too.

Samuel Butler

34. The Circle of Life

The first time Jingles and I went back to our neighborhood dog park after Ubee passed away, I thought about the circle of life. How does life go on when those we love die? We choose how to deal with losing loved ones. Some people put memories away and go on about their lives, while others hang on to loved ones by the strong thread of frequent memories. There is no right or wrong response.

The absence of a loved one always changes your life. Things will never be the same. But you can find ways to go on. I find great comfort when I close my eyes and think of my loved ones in happier times—like Ubee at the dog park.

We always carry those we love in our hearts. That doesn't change. To the loved ones who have gone on, thank you for loving us and making a difference in our lives. We will never forget you.

Love the animals: God has given
them the rudiments of thought
and joy untroubled.

Fyodor Dostoyevsky

35. Love Everything!

A very famous country western singer is a loveable guy. Every time I see him in concert, being interviewed, or cooking as a celebrity chef, he wears something that says "love" on it. The message is loud and clear from his outrageous top hat, T-shirt, and guitar: The words "Love everything" shine. If he were a dog (a great compliment), I think he would be a golden retriever. Goldens are so big and sweet and show love to everyone they encounter.

Messages like this, from one person to another, can create positive effects for everyone. Think about it...love everything. Wouldn't this world be a better place if we all tried to love everything? My dad had a little picture that said: "If people loved people the way dogs love people, there would be a lot of wet faces!" Today follow one of my country favorites...and all the dogs we know...and love everything.

36. Work Hard, Play Hard

Most dogs don't distinguish between working and playing. If you've ever seen agility competitions for dogs, you know what I mean. The dogs and their humans are put to the test by getting through various obstacles with a clock ticking away. It's a blast to watch these competitions because the dogs are working so hard and having so much fun doing it. The humans, while having fun, are really getting a workout.

I work with a group of physicians who really know how to work hard and play hard. They are totally devoted to providing excellent patient care, but on their time off they are out playing. Wow, can those guys play. They do everything from hiking and biking to extreme sports like Ironman competitions and even a few agility courses with their dogs.

Work some, play some. Find the right balance.

37. A Little Kindness

Such a sense of acceptance envelops us when dogs eagerly come up to say hello and to invite pats on the head or scratches of the ears and chin. About three-quarters of dogs readily greet the people who cross their paths. The other fourth growl or shy away. When you love animals, you want every dog to accept you, but no matter how hard you try, there are some who can't be won over with kind words or even a treat.

So it is with some people you will encounter. Not everybody will like you or want to get to know you. Have you taken this personally in the past? I know I have. But then I realized that a person's emotional distance or protective nature most often relates to how his or her life has unfolded. Many difficulties occur on life's road and damage happens. People and dogs get broken and become more guarded. The best thing to do is smile and greet each person and pup with the gift of kindness. You never know...one day they might greet you in return.

The purity of a person's heart can be quickly
measured by how they regard animals.

Anonymous

79

38. Be Strong

Abby is a beautiful Siberian husky that lives with my friends Bob and Cindy. They've had Abby (Abby-Abby as I call her) since she was a pup. She is a shining example of her breed—faithful, loving, playful, strong, and tough. Siberians can literally live in subdegree areas of the world without a problem. They have the original "thick skin."

As Abby has aged, so has her health. Not so long ago she developed diabetes. Bob and Cindy knew she wasn't quite right when they took her to the vet before receiving this diagnosis. What they didn't know was that she had also become blind. This big, beautiful dog, with the help of her other four-legged friends, was a great pretender. She made her humans think she had no problem seeing. The other dogs helped her along the way and her familiarity with her area contributed a lot as well. Talk about resilience!

We are fortunate when we meet people with a "be strong, be tough" mantra. My dear friend Thomas has to spend too many hours of his golden years going to doctor appointments, but his attitude remains strong and his giving spirit shines. At a point when many would have their visions of life clouded by disappointment, Thomas clearly sees the joy in being alive. That's true resilience.

Recollect that the Almighty,
who gave the dog to be
companion of our pleasures
and our toils, hath invested
him with a nature noble
and incapable of deceit.

Sir Walter Scott

39. Gratefulness

Dogs, no matter what their living environment, practice gratefulness every day. Many have lived through bad situations and then go on to live in happy, loving homes. I think dogs were created with a grateful gene.

Humans, on the other hand, are random about being grateful. Some don't practice it at all. They have no concept of blessings and good fortune. They believe they deserve all good things. But, like dogs, many people have been in bad situations and have lived through them. These people seem to appreciate more the good that comes to them. And like dogs, they are grateful each day for the blessings in their lives.

How grateful have you been lately? Stop for a moment and give thanks for all the good in your life. And if you're faced with trouble, remember all the good. Keep thanking God for every blessing. Soon there will be more than you can count.

40. No Good Can Come When You're Hot Under the Collar!

Sometimes when Jingles and I are on our evening walks, we encounter dogs that immediately want to beat Jingles up. Their temperament goes from hot to boiling instantly. They don't even know that Jingles wants to be their friend. They have already sized him up, judged him, and are ready to fight.

I'm sure you've witnessed people who are hot under the collar. They go through life ready to attack before they understand the other person's viewpoint. Some people will shrug this off and say that's just the way they are. I say, "Yikes!" Who can live or work with people who are like this? And who wants to?

When you encounter a collar on fire in both the dog world and the people world...try to extinguish it with your own attitude. If that doesn't work, head for the waterpark!

41. Take Time to Play

In a dog's life there is always time to stop and play. They have well-placed priorities. When was the last time you did something that gave you pure enjoyment, laughter from deep inside, and contentment?

A friend and I love to look at houses. She likes the interiors, while I am constantly in awe of beautiful gardens, water features, and flowers. An hour or two of this refreshes both of us and gives us great ideas for future projects.

Some of my friends have campers and hit the road whenever possible. This is their ultimate act of play. They have very busy lives, but they realize a respite helps them to keep up day to day.

Get out there and play. Do something you've always wanted to do. And while you're playing, throw the ball for the cat or the dog—their appreciation will be an additional reward for playing.

42. Try to See the Other Side

Jingles loves the dog park. In his older age, he's good about hanging close to me. When Ubee was still with us, she was just the opposite. As soon as she hit the gate she was partying and socializing with the other dogs. Dogs have a great sense of what dogs to be friendly with and which ones they should just pass on. The very athletic dogs that were into catching the ball and running a lot stayed away from Ubee, while shy dogs steered away from her happy, rambunctious ways as well. There were always lots of dogs to get to know. Dogs are also good about sorting out humans—those who will accept them and those who would rather the dogs just keep on going.

People are a lot like this. Introvert? Extrovert? Some enjoy being the center of attention and consider everyone a friend, some are more comfortable being in the corner, while still others like a little of both worlds. It's nice when people can accept the qualities and personalities of others. It really does make all of our lives more rounded when we know people with traits similar and dissimilar to our own.

Once in a while step into the other part of the party. It's just as fun to observe as it is to participate. Enjoy the celebration in your unique way.

43. Jobs

Dogs have many jobs. They are, of course, all on friend duty for their humans. Other dogs have bigger jobs outside the home, such as leading the blind, sniffing out bombs and drugs at ports, and protecting our soldiers at war. No matter what their responsibilities are, a dog is a great co-worker for their human partners even when work conditions are tough—like when they are homeless.

Rusty is a dog with a sunshine coat and heart of gold for his human, Mark. Every day Rusty and Mark stand on a corner of town where there is a huge amount of foot and vehicle traffic. These two have been on that corner day in and day out since I moved here six years ago. In the heat, rain, snow, and bitter cold, you will find them there. They work more hours a day and in the week than the average worker in an office does. It goes without saying that they have a hard life, but they make the best of it.

Over the years I have come to know these two and the signs they carry—always pointing out that the dog is family and the human does not do drugs or drink. Circumstances have caused their lot, and you would be hard pressed to find a more positive human in such a cruel environment. Mark makes no excuses for the way he lives, and he is always grateful for what people give him. Many give the dog sweaters, hats, and even sunglasses—humor in the hardest of circumstances.

When Monday morning rolls around and you're dreading leaving your nice, comfortable home for that warm office that has great coffee, remember Rusty and Mark out on the streets. Remind yourself that life can be viewed as work, as labor, as struggle...or it can be experienced as an opportunity to be grateful for your little corner of the world.

One of the saddest of sights in a world of sin
is the little lost pup with his tail tucked in.

Arthur Guiterman

44. Explore New Places

The discovery of new places can be so much fun. You'll be amazed how going 15 to 20 minutes from your front door can reveal a whole new adventure. When I first moved to my new town, I went out and about every Sunday. I found amazing views, vineyards, farms, and small towns. It made me less homesick because they reminded me so much of home, yet they were unique and full of new possibilities as well.

Dogs love exploring every square inch of a new place—new trees, grasses, and yards. Oh, how they love the new smells! Do yourself a favor and take a drive or walk beyond your normal life route this weekend. You might find an unknown lake, a country road that leads to a magnificent waterfall, or a roadside produce stand that refreshes your mind and body. Ahhh! So what are you waiting for?

A watchdog is a dog
kept to guard your home,
usually by sleeping
where a burglar would
awaken the household
by falling over him.

Anonymous

45. Lazy Days

Have you ever wondered why the hot, lazy, summer days are described as "dog days"? I found the answer recently. Dog lovers will find this fascinating.

In ancient times people drew images in the sky by mentally "connecting the dots" of the stars. These star pictures are now called constellations. The Romans saw images of bears (Ursa Major and Ursa Minor), twins (Gemini), a bull (Taurus), and others, including dogs (Canis Major and Canis Minor).

The brightest of the stars in Canis Major (the big dog) is Sirius, which also happens to be the brightest star in the night sky. However, in the summer, Sirius, the "dog star," rises and sets with the sun. During late July, Sirius is in conjunction with the sun, and the Romans believed that its heat added to the heat of the sun, creating a stretch of hot and sultry weather. They named this period of time, from 20 days before the conjunction to 20 days after, "dog days" after the dog star.

Now that sets the record straight that all dogs are indeed stars!

The warmth of summer makes us forget months of bad weather. Jingles doesn't ponder how he shivered during our evening winter walks. Instead he lies around, delighted to stretch, yawn, sip some fresh water, and then lie right back down again.

I know a lot of people who savor the dog days as well. It's a time to take it easy and have fun with friends. The barbecue is calling out. Bring on some cold drinks and potato salad. I'm sure at some point during the next round of dog days we'll all look up to the sky and search for that dog star that truly tells us it is summer.

46. Thirsty

At the dog park there are endless opportunities for the dogs to quench their thirst and jump into the cooling sensation of water. Some dogs will run and slide into a wading pool and accomplish two tasks, cooling themselves off and having a drink of water at the same time. And most of the time they're not alone in that pool. It just seems automatic that other dogs should join them. They don't hesitate to share their rain puddles, pools, or bowls of water.

We deal with many types of thirst. When it is a physical thirst, we can enjoy our favorite refreshment. When it is a deeper thirst for love, success, and acceptance, it's not always as easy to quench. However, it is amazing how one can be refreshed on the inside and out by sharing. Do what dogs do— share a big bowl of life with others. Your thirst will be greatly satisfied.

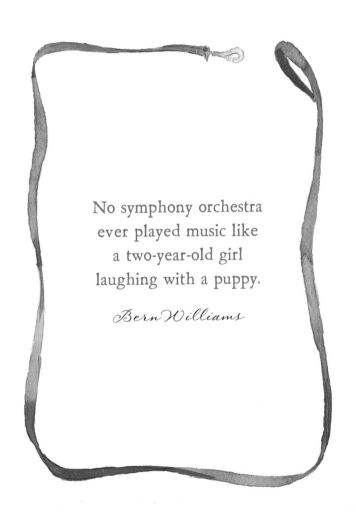

No symphony orchestra
ever played music like
a two-year-old girl
laughing with a puppy.

Bern Williams

47. Get Excited

When dogs get excited their whole bodies show it:
Wags erupt from their noses to their tails. They don't hide
their emotions behind pretense or attitude. They are never
too cool to leap with absolute delight and shake, shake,
shake with happiness.

I will always remember the day my friend and agent
came running into my office to tell me about a book contract.
Her pure excitement started at the top of her head and went
down to her toes. We were dancing around, laughing, crying,
and expressing our joy so openly that all of my co-workers
came and joined in.

Excitement and absolute joy are very good for us.
When the chance for that kind of happiness comes upon
you or crosses your path, absorb the wonder of it and,
for a brief moment, put everything else aside.

48. Greetings

Recently I was reunited with three girlfriends. When they arrived at the airport, I could hardly contain my excitement at being together again after several years. We all agreed it had been way too long. The moment I saw them, I ran to them with my arms out, just like you see in the movies...or at the dog park.

When my friend Eddie comes to visit, he always brings his adorable Boston terrier, Patton. When Jingles and Patton see each other, we basically have to clear out of their way as these two canine pals run, collide, sniff, and play. They'll have a ball for hours until they crash for naps. As soon as they wake up, they start all over again. They don't get caught up in worries about a future parting; they enjoy the present moment and the chance to share it.

Next time you greet old friends, run to them and savor the time you get to spend together.

Dogs laugh, but they laugh with their tails.

Max Eastman

49. Comfort Zone

Some dogs have to go through many homes before they really find the right place. It's a sad fact that some people don't understand the commitment that comes with being a pet parent (any kind of parent for that matter). Dogs that are passed from home to home (or home to shelter to home) get confused and scared. They started out life having a comfort zone they understand. Then things change on them. Many dogs are able to adapt after a short time of love and care. Some struggle to warm up when comfort zones change.

Remember the first time you went to swim lessons? Perhaps you were brave and just jumped in. Or maybe you were like me, not ready to jump in or step out of my comfort zone. I eventually jumped in, but I didn't like it. I had a hard time warming up to the idea—to this day I am not a fan of the water.

There are times we have to leave our comfort zone and enter places or situations we have never experienced. If we have support, these can be our chances to blossom and find better ways of living. Our dog friends need this same encouragement as they face new beginnings. If you are one of those people lucky enough to offer a comfort zone to a pup or an older dog, remember that we all need an extra dose of nurturing when we face change.

50. The Seasons of Change

With the first sighting of a big, orange, full moon we all know that fall has arrived. The air is brisk as summer bids adieu and that big moon lights up the night. Big airplanes fly over my house and get no attention from the dogs. But a big, golden moon brings out their true canine behavior. The dogs want to stay outside more. My dogs even exchange their soft indoor beds for blankets of grass. They know that this new, big moon signals their chance to ease out of one season and welcome another.

I too love the big, autumn moon. I can feel the change in the temperature—time to think about adding another blanket to the bed, putting summer clothes away, and getting out some sweaters. Where are those rain shoes?

Sometimes we humans want to hang on to certain seasons because they do something special for us, for our spirits. My nephew loves the summer because he can get out there and hike. The change of seasons means there are less of those days left for adventures. Many of my friends live in areas where there are a great number of sunny days, so they welcome the rain when it comes. (I would like to send them some showers from the Northwest!)

Every season is special. This truth helps those of us who resist change to segue into the new wonders a different season brings with it. We can't help but notice the change in the air, moon, earth, people, and dogs around us. Open your arms to the seasons of the year and the seasons of life. Honor change for the good that happens when we welcome something new and different to our lives.

51. Sometimes It Isn't Fun Being Top Dog!

Top dogs have tough jobs. The leader of the pack always carries the heavier load. For instance, consider the dogs that run in the Iditarod. The lead dog has such a big job keeping everyone and everything on track. He must watch the road, maneuver over rough terrain, break the snow, obey commands, and pull his weight 100 percent of the time.

In our lives, top dogs such as bosses, supervisors, and coaches pull a heavy weight for the team. Good bosses lead by example and dedication as they carry out responsibilities for the team, the clients, and the bottom-line needs. Like lead dogs, most bosses love what they do, and many find that their passion drives them.

Today, put yourself in the shoes or paws of the top dogs. Help them out a little more than usual. For sure, their ears will perk up—and if the two-legged top dog had a tail, it would be wagging.

If a dog will not come
to you after having looked
you in the face,
you should go home and
examine your conscience.

Woodrow Wilson

52. Stop and Smell Nature

Have you ever noticed that the first thing a dog usually does when he steps outside in the morning is put his nose in the air and smell nature? I'd like to ask them why they do that first thing, and what they smell when they sniff the air. My theory is that they like to know everything is where it's supposed to be (well, and that there are no intruders on their property).

When was the last time you stopped to take in a big breath of fresh air? To look around at life and appreciate the blessings and the balance? We're so quick to step out our doors and into our busy lives that we sometimes miss the joy that can be found smelling the autumn air, spring flowers, or summertime breezes. Pausing for a moment of gratitude refreshes you for the day ahead and supplies you with the reserve of calm and peace that you need throughout the busy day.

53. Always Live in the Positive

Snuffy the bassett hound came to live with us during a time when my dad really needed a friend. His health was failing, and so was the memory of his life and who his family was. Snuffy's road to reach our lives was not an easy one. His past owner had purchased him to show and breed. But when it was clear that Snuffy didn't want to be a show dog, and it was discovered that due to overbreeding in his family line he was unable to be a father, that owner neglected the sweet bassett.

Snuffy tried escaping many times. You have to wonder if there are angels looking out for our canine friends because Snuffy's house was not far from the 101 Freeway in California. Many times he ended up walking along the freeway. Thankfully he always survived, but sadly, the owner always brought him back to the unhappy home where two large dogs terrorized Snuffy. Finally the owner must've tired of this game of fetch, so she called the Humane Society to enlist help in finding Snuffy a new home.

Well, Snuffy had a higher calling than merely being a show dog! He wanted to love and be loved. When he came to live with us, he took to my dad in an instant. You would have thought that his past would've left him scared and scarred and unable to trust a human. But somehow he had the ability to keep loving.

How many times do we hear stories about people blaming their actions on their lots in life? We all experience bad things throughout our lives and times when we are stranded on a freeway of worry, unable to discern which way will lead us to safety. When this happens to me, I raise my hands to the Lord and immediately know the way to go. There is always a way out of the darkness. And there is always a home worth waiting for. Snuffy is sure of it!

54. Run...Run...and Keep on Running!

During my many visits to the dog park I have observed that young pups and senior dogs share the same prescription for a happy life: Run, run, and keep on running! The dogs know instinctively that keeping their minds and bodies as active as possible will keep them in the race. There may be bumps in the road and branches on the path they must hurdle and navigate, but their momentum and eagerness carry them through.

We can do this too. When troubles such as debt, job stress, family struggles, and health issues weigh us down, we can choose to give up or rise up and keep running. Fueled by faith and hope, we can hurdle those problems, get around them, or avoid them altogether. It just requires a first step. There you go! That wasn't so hard. Now step again...and again... keep going...keep going...

55. Beauty Is More Than What You See

In surveying the many cute, endearing, and regal faces among the dog park puppy crowd, I've found that it's often the scruffiest-looking dogs who radiate the most personality. A purebred might have a nobler nose or the quickest gait, but a pedigree doesn't guarantee that you will have friends.

How many times have you heard someone comment on another person's appearance and equate it to his or her value? Yes, the act of judging can be very useful. I think judging cookies, cakes, and breads at the county fair is a fine thing to do. However, using judgment to rate people is not so useful. If we glance at people's appearances (or their résumés) and make our decisions about who they are and whether or not we should be their friends, we are missing out on the most wonderful people God is placing in our lives.

Take a little more time to truly see the people around you. Make the effort to witness internal beauty. Engage in conversation and show that you care about every person as an individual. You'll be amazed at the warm, fun, and charming personalities you will encounter.

Every boy should have two things:
a dog and a mother
willing to let him have one.

Anonymous

56. Pass Along Happiness

When dogs meet up nose to nose, I believe they are saying hello and accepting one another. This cordial greeting seems to inspire a dog to move on to yet another new or old friend and say hello. They pass along happiness to other dogs, and we know they pass along happiness to us. There is nothing better than being entertained by a four-legged friend. You just have to sit back, smile, and enjoy the company of a dear pal.

Years ago I lived in a neighborhood that was very culturally diverse. Many of the people were strawberry workers. These folks worked hard and didn't have much. One family had an old house they worked on every hour they were not working in the fields. Every night when I came home there was a bag of strawberries fresh from the field that day on my doorknob. It was such a thoughtful gift. I would wave and say, "thank you."

I kept wondering what I could do in return with my limited resources. So one Saturday morning I got up and made chocolate chip cookies and tuna fish sandwiches—three dozen of each, as there were many adults and children living in the old, small house. As soon as I saw them come home, I took over my gift. They were so happy about my offering. Our conversation was limited due to the language barrier, but the universal language of love and kindness was spoken.

I looked out my window a little later, and they were all gathered in a circle—adults and children—eating the lunch I'd prepared for them. There was no barbecue, no long buffet... it was even better because there was a family sharing time and food together.

When was the last time you received or passed along happiness? I hope your answer comes quickly with a strong sense of those moments of receiving and then giving joy. One can never pass along too much happiness.

57. Never Let a Little Rain Get You Down

Winter at the dog park is a muddy mess. Only extreme dogs and people venture there during this time. Usually the dogs hanging out at the dog park in the winter are the water dogs such as Labs, retrievers, and little dogs like Jingles who like investigating nooks and crannies of winter's tall grasses and fallen tree branches.

If you and your dog are not explorers, it's far more tempting to curl up on the couch in front of a roaring fire during the wet seasons. My advice to you? Just once do what extreme dogs and their humans do during the winter and get outside!

I've known this secret for some time...dogs surely created Slip 'N Slides. Go ahead, let the fun, mud, and sliding begin. The discoveries beyond your stoop are vast and rewarding... even when the clouds are overhead.

Money will buy you a pretty good dog,
but it won't buy you the wag of his tail.

Author Unknown

58. Sometimes You Lead...

There is a saying that if you aren't the lead dog, the scenery all looks the same. We can't ask the dogs, but I think they would disagree with this statement. Just like us, these great animals see life from different eyes so the scenery is different. There is a new dog park in our neighborhood. There are no defined paths carved out in the landscape yet. It is up to the dogs to create them. I'm sure some will lead, some will follow, and then some special ones will go off on their own and start new paths. Most will allow their noses to take them on their adventures. You can't stop a dog from adventuring!

A great cattle trail was first created by wild animals. Then came the livestock and horses. It was further set in the countryside and through mountain ranges by wagons and humans. The trail eventually became a road and then a superhighway. Aren't you amazed at the pioneers who shaped lasting paths in their pursuit of new homes and better lives? The labor and the losses were great, but the life they were carving out for themselves and for future generations was even greater.

There will always be those who lead the way and make the trail of life wider, easier, and better for everyone. Then there will be those who follow the leaders. And then there are those special ones who are adventurous and go off the path to create new and better ones for us. I believe at one time or another we all get a chance to be a leader, a follower, and a trailblazer. No matter our role at the particular time, when we find our stride, we'll find our path and our way through life.

59. Grab Life!

How fun to see dogs riding in cars with their heads hanging out the window, gulping the breezes that rush by their eager faces. That is really catching a breath of fresh air! Jingles loves riding in the car. He sits in the middle and seems convinced he is helping me drive. He is alert and happy and clearly loving life. We might think this simple pleasure is purely for the dogs. We are humans, and we need to provide and make plans and work. Who has time for pure pleasure?

Growing up in farm country, there were always lots of working dogs. Farm dogs truly love their jobs—jumping in the truck, helping set pipe, being on the front line at harvest time, putting in hours day and night. Wind in their hair and sun on their faces, they're drinking in all life has to offer. These dogs are grabbing life with their paws and hanging on.

We have moments of great enthusiasm, but we could have more. We forget to watch for joy to come our way or we forget that we can create joy with our attitudes and perspectives and beliefs in blessings. When we awaken to ways to live remarkably, we will discover how to gulp in this amazing life and grab the gusto of happiness before it passes us by.

Dogs' lives are too short.
Their only fault, really.

Agnes Sligh Turnbull

60. Be Nice

Nice dogs always get in the door; mean dogs have to stay out. We all know that mean dogs don't just happen. Lack of food, love, and comfort can make a dog pretty mean. Many times human behavior has caused the bad temperament in an animal.

I've never understood people who choose not to be nice. We all encounter them at one time or another. Sometimes these people refuse to accept nice people into their lives. Their baggage is heavy with resentment and usually an unforgiving, hardened heart.

My choice and the choice of all those I love (including four-legged ones) is to be nice to everyone. How our efforts of kindness are accepted is not up to us. Nice people will always accept nice people.

Now, what to do with those not-so-nice people? I think we should pray for them right now. Perhaps with our prayers and the warmth of our hearts and smiles we might win over a not-so-nice person and bring out the more compassionate person that is waiting to get out from beneath the shell of indifference. Can it be as simple as "Be nice"? Truly it can.

When you feel lousy,
puppy therapy is indicated.

Sara Paretsky

61. Just Be Brave

"Just be brave" was the first entry I made in my journal while visiting the dog park. How fitting that it should be the last entry in this book. It's hard for dogs to go into new territory. They are overwhelmed by all the new smells and by a host of dogs that may or may not be accepting and pleasant.

We humans face this every day. The minute we leave our homes and head out into the world there will be people who accept us and those who won't. There will be muddy potholes to get through and sunny days to bask in. Hopefully there will be more sun than mud for you.

Every day we choose to live life to its fullest. Be thankful for all of your blessings and be brave throughout the journey. By and large it is a great journey, isn't it!

Heaven goes by favour.
If it went by merit, you would
stay out and your dog would go in.

Mark Twain

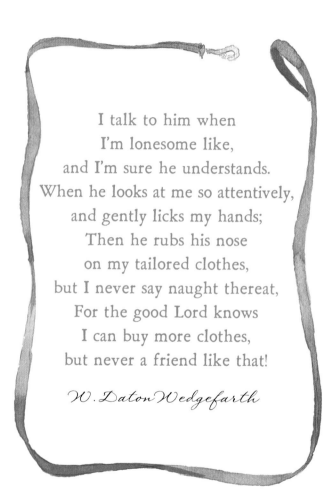

I talk to him when
I'm lonesome like,
and I'm sure he understands.
When he looks at me so attentively,
and gently licks my hands;
Then he rubs his nose
on my tailored clothes,
but I never say naught thereat,
For the good Lord knows
I can buy more clothes,
but never a friend like that!

W. Daton Wedgefarth

128